The Mighty Ark
and other poems

Compiled by
John Foster

OXFORD
UNIVERSITY PRESS

OXFORD
UNIVERSITY PRESS

Great Clarendon Street, Oxford OX2 6DP

Oxford University Press is a department of the University of Oxford.
It furthers the University's objective of excellence in research, scholarship,
and education by publishing worldwide in

Oxford New York
Athens Auckland Bangkok Bogotá Buenos Aires Calcutta
Cape Town Chennai Dar es Salaam Delhi Florence Hong Kong Istanbul
Karachi Kuala Lumpur Madrid Melbourne Mexico City Mumbai
Nairobi Paris São Paulo Singapore Taipei Tokyo Toronto Warsaw

and associated companies in Berlin Ibadan

Oxford is a trade mark of Oxford University Press
in the UK and in certain other countries

© Oxford University Press 2000
First published 2000

All rights reserved
You must not circulate this book in any other binding or cover
and you must impose this same condition on any acquiror

British Library Cataloguing in Publication Data
Data available

ISBN 0 19 917284 6

Printed in Hong Kong

The editor and publisher would like to thank pupils of Batt CE Primary School, Witney and Oxford High School Junior Department for their help with comments on the poems.

The National Literacy Strategy termly requirements for poetry at Year 3 are fulfilled on the following pages:

Term 1

pp 5–15, 20, 28–29, 34–37, 40–48.

Term 2

pp 13, 18, 24–26, 30–33.

Term 3

pp 16, 22, 38–39, 50–60.

For more detailed information on the poetry range requirements and the termly objectives, see Oxford Literacy Web Poetry Teacher's Guide 1.

Contents

Silver	*Walter de la Mare*	5
Moon	*Ann Bonner*	6
Who Has Seen the Wind?	*Christina Rossetti*	8
Butterflies	*N C Wickramasinghe*	8
On a Breezy Day	*Iain Crichton-Smith*	9
The Wind	*James Reeves*	9
Balloon	*Colleen Thibaudeau*	10
Ambitious Aeroplane	*Gina Douthwaite*	11
Definitions	*John Cotton*	12
My Sari	*Debjani Chatterjee*	13
I Asked the Little Boy Who Cannot See	*Anon*	14
Pink is a Marshmallow Whisper	*Celia Warren*	15
J is for Jazz-man	*Eleanor Farjeon*	16
I Love the	*Marc Matthews*	18
The Alleyway	*Richard Edwards*	20
As I was Coming to School	*Allan Ahlberg*	22
Granny Granny Please Comb My Hair	*Grace Nichols*	24
I Like to Stay Up	*Grace Nichols*	26
Fishes' Evening Song	*Dahlov Ipcar*	28
Sea Fever	*John Masefield*	29
The Mighty Ark	*Jack Ousbey*	30
I'm a Parrot	*Grace Nichols*	34

Badgers	*Richard Edwards*	36
At the Bottom of the Garden	*Grace Nichols*	37
Squirrel	*Ted Hughes*	37
Giraffes	*Mary Ann Hoberman*	38
The Panther	*Ogden Nash*	39
The Year	*Julie Holder*	40
Recipe for Spring	*Joan Poulson*	41
Fireworks	*Steve Turner*	42
Autumn is…	*Andrew Collett*	43
Winter	*John Foster*	44
December Leaves	*Kaye Starbird*	45
The Greedy Monster	*Irene Rawnsley*	46
Dreamer	*Brian Moses*	48
A Letter to the Alphabet	*Julie Holder*	50
Rhythm Machine	*Trevor Harvey*	51
Guess Who Haiku (Creatures)	*Daphne Kitching*	52
Riddle Me Hot, Riddle Me Cold	*John Foster*	53
The Land of the Bumbley Boo	*Spike Milligan*	54
Tongue Twisters	*Colin West*	56
Shaun Short's Short Shorts	*John Foster*	57
A Famous Painter	*Anon*	58
There was an Old Man of Blackheath	*Anon*	58
Little Miss Fidget	*Bill Condon*	59
Some Favourite Words	*Richard Edwards*	60
Index of First lines		62
Acknowledgements		64

Silver

Slowly, silently, now the moon
Walks the night in her silver shoon;
This way, and that, she peers, and sees
Silver fruit upon silver trees;
One by one the casements catch
Her beams beneath the silvery thatch;
Couched in his kennel, like a log,
With paws of silver sleeps the dog;
From their shadowy cote the white breasts peep
Of doves in a silver-feathered sleep;
A harvest mouse goes scampering by,
With silver claws, and silver eye;
And moveless fish in the water gleam,
By silver reeds in a silver stream.

Walter de la Mare

This poem makes me think how magical moonlight is.

Moon

A white face
in the night.
A ten
pence piece
in the dark
of your pocket
shining
secretly bright.

A cold light
blue-circled
with winter's
frostbite.
A sliver
a shiver of ice.

A melon slice slung
in a sky spiced
with stars.
An ivory horn
still there
with the dawn.

And a great
golden plate
risen with dusk.
Coming to rest
low over fields
heavy
with harvest.

Ann Bonner

I like the way
this poem helps
you to picture
the moon.

Who Has Seen the Wind?

Who has seen the wind?
   Neither I nor you:
But when the leaves hang trembling,
   The wind is passing through.

Who has seen the wind?
   Neither you nor I:
But when the leaves bow down their heads,
   The wind is passing by.

Christina Rossetti

Butterflies

Butterflies:
Like pieces of torn paper
Strewn into the wind.

N C Wickramasinghe

On a Breezy Day

On a breezy day
the curtains swell at the window
like white ghosts
that are struggling to get out.

Iain Crichton-Smith

The Wind

I can get through a doorway without any key,
And strip the leaves from the great oak tree.
I can drive storm clouds and shake tall towers,
Or steal through a garden and not wake the flowers.
Seas I can move and ships I can sink;
I can carry a house-top or the scent of a pink.
When I am angry I can rave and riot;
And when I am spent, I lie quiet as quiet.

James Reeves

Balloon

as big as ball as round as sun ... I tug and pull you when you run and when wind blows I say politely

H
O
L
D
M
E
T
I
G
H
T
L
Y.

Colleen Thibaudeau

> This reminds me of when I lost a balloon on a windy day.

Ambitious Aeroplane

An aeroplane climbs up its vapour trail ladder to the top of the sky

Gina Douthwaite

I enjoyed working out how to read this.

Definitions

Banana

A custard coloured
Sweet smile,
New Moon,
Tasty telephone,
Bouncy boat,
And a slippery end!

Cherries

Eatable ear-rings,
Mouthwatering marbles,
Bright beads,
Cheerful cheeks,
Rosy pebbles,
Fortune tellers.

Eyes

Small reed fringed pools,
Miniature mirrors,
The head's windows,
Letters in of light,
Glistening charmers.

John Cotton

My Sari

Saris hang on the washing line:
a rainbow in our neighbourhood.
This little orange one is mine,
it has a mango leaf design.
I wear it as a Rani would.
It wraps around me like sunshine,
it ripples silky down my spine,
and I stand tall and feel so good.

Debjani Chatterjee

I feel like this when I wear my sari.

I Asked the Little Boy Who Cannot See

I asked the little boy who cannot see,
"And what is colour like?"
"Why, green," said he,
"Is like the rustle when the wind blows through
The forest; running water, that is blue;
And red is like a trumpet sound; and pink
Is like the smell of roses; and I think
That purple must be like a thunderstorm;
And yellow is like something soft and warm;
And white is a pleasant stillness when you lie
And dream."

Anon

This helped me to understand what it's like to be blind.

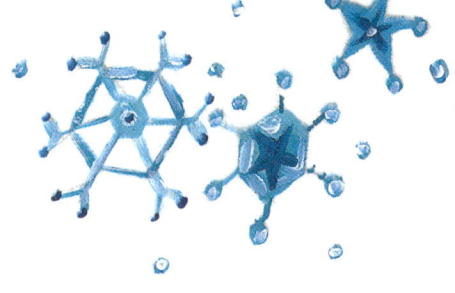

Pink is a Marshmallow Whisper

pink is a marshmallow whisper
black is a dream in a cave
green is a gossiping goblin
red is heart that is brave
yellow is streaming pleasure
blue is freezing despair
purple's a painful hollow
orange a slice of care
grey is a shivering shadow
white is a crackling wish
brown is melted winter
silver's a miracle fish
gold is a loving handshake
bronze is a song without words
turquoise is pebbles of laughter
crimson's a nestful of birds

Celia Warren

J is for Jazz-man

Crash and
    CLANG!
Bash and
    BANG!

And up in the road the Jazz-man sprang!
The One-Man-Jazz-Band playing in the street,
Drums with his Elbows, Cymbals with his Feet,
Pipes with his Mouth, Accordion with his Hand,
Playing all his instruments to Beat the Band!

TOOT and
        Tingle!
HOOT and
        Jingle!

Oh, what a clatter! How the tunes all mingle!
Twenty Children couldn't make as much Noise as
The Howling Pandemonium of the One-Man-Jazz!

Eleanor Farjeon

> The rhyme and rhythms help me hear the one-man band.

I Love the

friday night smell of mammie baking bread – creeping up to me in bed, and tho zzzz I'll fall asleep, before I even get a bite – when morning come, you can bet I'll meet a kitchen table laden with bread, still warm and fresh salt bread sweet bread crisp and brown and best of all coconut buns THAT's why I love the friday night smell of mammie baking bread

putting me to
sleep, dreaming
of jumping from
the highest branch
of the jamoon tree
into the red water
creek
beating calton
run and catching
the biggest fish
in the world
plus, getting
the answers right
to every single
sum
that every day
in my dream
begins and ends
with the friday
night smell of
mammie baking
bread, and
coconut buns
of course.

Marc Matthews

This reminds me of
my Gran's baking.

The Alleyway

The alleyway is crooked,
The alleyway is damp,
The alleyway has corners,
Untouched by any lamp,
The alleyway has bats in
And ghosts and thieves and rats in,
So please don't make me
Please don't make me
Please don't make me
Please don't make me
Please don't make me walk the alleyway.

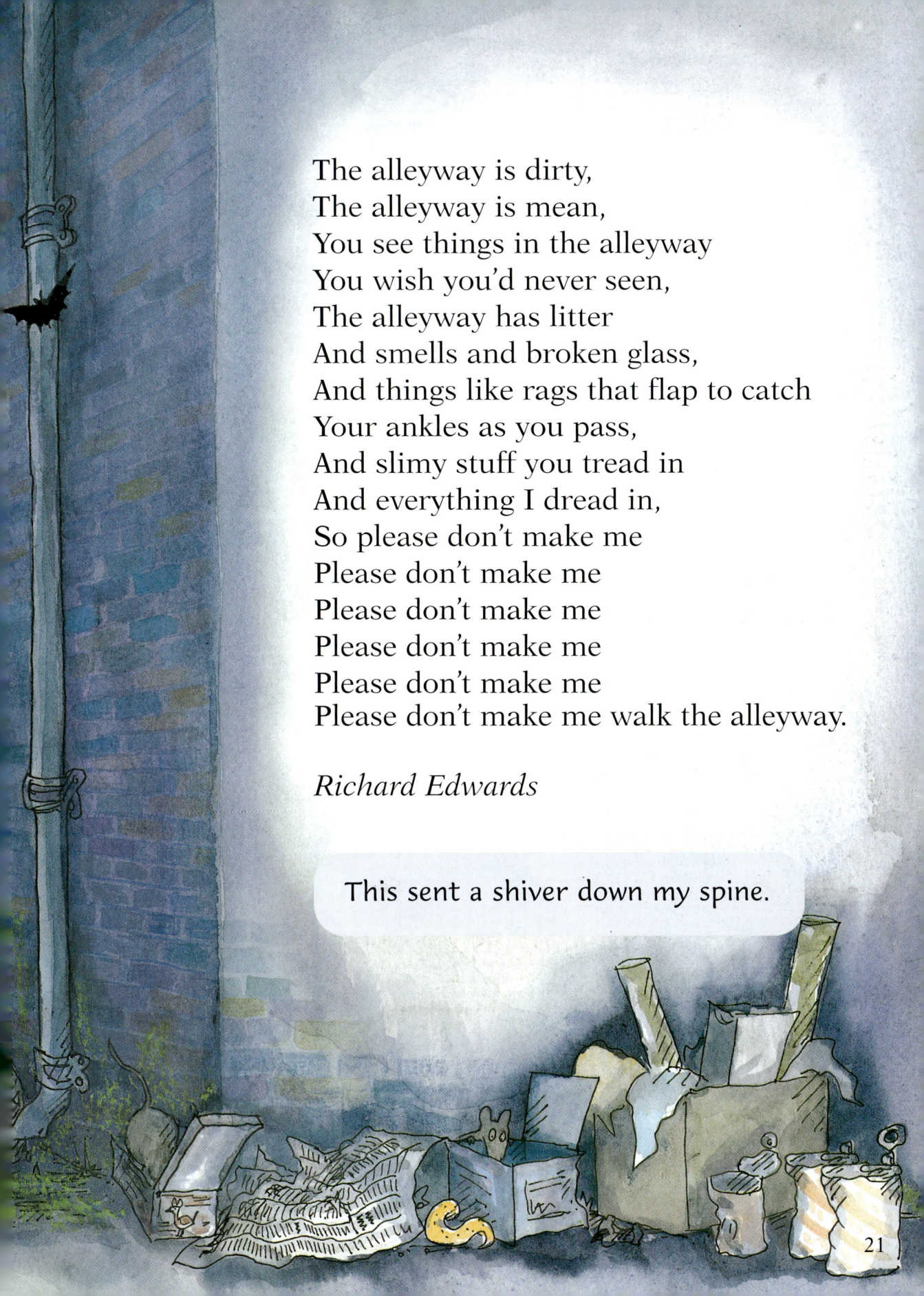

The alleyway is dirty,
The alleyway is mean,
You see things in the alleyway
You wish you'd never seen,
The alleyway has litter
And smells and broken glass,
And things like rags that flap to catch
Your ankles as you pass,
And slimy stuff you tread in
And everything I dread in,
So please don't make me
Please don't make me
Please don't make me
Please don't make me
Please don't make me
Please don't make me walk the alleyway.

Richard Edwards

This sent a shiver down my spine.

As I was Coming to School

As I was coming to school, Sir,
To learn my ABC,
I was picked up and put in a sack, Sir,
And carried off on his back, Sir,
By a Russian who took me to sea.

So I had to swim all the way back, Sir,
And I still had my legs in the sack, Sir,
And the waves were forty foot high, Sir,
Which is really the reason why, Sir –
I would not tell a lie, Sir –
I'm late for school today.

Is it all right to go out to play?

Allan Ahlberg

Granny Granny Please Comb My Hair

Granny Granny
please comb my hair
you always take your time
you always take such care

You put me to sit on a cushion
between your knees
you rub a little coconut oil
parting gentle as a breeze.

Mummy Mummy
she's always in a hurry-hurry
rush
she pulls my hair
sometimes she tugs

But Granny
you have all the time in the world
and when you're finished
you always turn my head and say
"Now who's a nice girl."

Grace Nichols

It's just what it's like when my Gran does my hair.

I Like to Stay Up

I like to stay up
and listen
when big people talking
jumbie stories

I does feel
so tingly and excited
inside me

But when my mother say,
'Girl, time for bed'

Then is when
I does feel a dread

Then is when
I does jump into me bed

Then is when
I does cover up
from me feet to me head

Then is when
I does wish I didn't listen
to no stupid jumbie story

Then is when
I does wish I did read
me book instead

Grace Nichols

('Jumbie' is a Guyanese word for 'ghost'.)

That's how I feel when I've heard a scary story.

Fishes' Evening Song

Flip flop,
Flip flap,
Slip slap,
Lip lap;
Water sounds,
Soothing sounds.
We fan our fins
As we lie
Resting here
Eye to eye.
Water falls
Drop by drop,
Plip plop,
Drip drop.
Plink plunk,
Splash splish;
Fish fins fan,
Fish tails swish,
Swush, swash, swish.
This we wish…
Water cold,
Water clear,
Water smooth,
Just to soothe
Sleepy fish.

Dahlov Ipcar

Sea Fever

I must go down to the seas again,
   to the lonely sea and the sky,
And all I ask is a tall ship and a star to steer her by,
And the wheel's kick and the wind's song
   and the white sails shaking,
And a grey mist on the sea's face and a grey dawn breaking.

I must go down to the seas again,
   for the call of the running tide
Is a wild call and a clear call that may not be denied;
And all I ask is a windy day with the white clouds flying,
And the flung spray and the blown spume,
   and the seagulls crying.

I must go down to the seas again, to the vagrant gypsy life,
To the gull's way and the whale's way
   where the wind's like a whetted-knife
And all I ask is a merry yarn from a laughing fellow-rover,
And a quiet sleep and a sweet dream
   when the long trick's over.

John Masefield

The Mighty Ark

When the rain first started it was just a shower
And the Lord called down and he said to Noah:
Work in the daylight and work in the dark,
And build out of gopher wood a mighty big Ark.
The waters will be rolling and the flood will come
They'll wash away your farm and submerge your home.
Listen Mr Noah you can make your mark:
If you work for the Lord and you build him an Ark.

    Ark, Ark, a mighty big Ark
    A wonderful, waterproof, mighty big Ark.

So he builded the Ark and he builded it sound,
And he called to the animals living around,
Come on you creatures, it's two of each kind,
I'm taking you in, leaving no one behind;
Birds and bears and buffaloes and bees,
Flamingos, fireflies and chicken fleas,
Glow worms, slow worms, kiwis, kites,
Natterjacks, polecats, moths and mites.

    Ark, Ark, a mighty big Ark
    A wonderful, waterproof, mighty big Ark.

And the rain came down, and it poured so hard
It covered Noah's home, made a river in his yard.
It swamped the fields, it topped the trees,
It turned small lakes into thundering seas.
Lightning flashed and the sky grew dark,
But the animals were dry on the mighty Ark.
And then Noah shouted to all on board,
Give thanks and remember the word of the Lord.

> Ark, Ark, a mighty big Ark
> A wonderful, waterproof, mighty big Ark.

After thirty days the rain stopped falling,
A day or two more and the wind stopped squalling.
But the waters were high and the sky was dark
And the one safe place was on Noah's Ark.
Then things brightened up, Noah raised his hand
And the dove flew off to search for land.
When they saw her again she was tired and weak
But she carried a twig of leaves in her beak.

> Ark, Ark, a mighty big Ark
> A wonderful, waterproof, mighty big Ark.

Noah then gave praise to the Lord above
And he told all the animals, We're on the move.
The flood is dying and the waters will be still,
And we'll beach the Ark on the side of that hill.
I'll tell you all, when we reach that place
I shall lift up my arms, I shall show my face
To the Lordy Lord, whose Kingdom come,
Who saved us all and brought us home.

> Ark, Ark, a mighty big Ark
> A wonderful, waterproof, mighty big Ark.

Then the camels and the cows and the kangaroos,
The bears and the hares and the caribous,
The pups, and cubs, the squabs and kids,
The reptiles, herbivores and arachnids,
Lacewings, ladybirds, wasps and bees
Thunderbugs, locusts and chicken fleas,
Noah and his wife and everyone on board
Left the mighty Ark in the keeping of the Lord.

    Ark, Ark, a mighty big Ark
    Wonderful, waterproof, mighty big Ark
    Ark, Ark, a mighty big Ark
    The absolutely wonderful
        positively waterproof
          world-shaking gopher wood
            thorough-going masterpiece
          mighty big unsinkable…
        ARK

Jack Ousbey

I'm a Parrot

I am a parrot
I live in a cage
I'm nearly always
in a vex-up rage

I used to fly
all light and free
in the luscious green
forest canopy

I am a parrot
I live in a cage
I'm nearly always
in a vex-up rage

I miss the wind
against my wing
I miss the nut
and the fruit picking

I am a parrot
I live in a cage
I'm nearly always
in a vex-up rage

I squalk I talk
I curse I swear
I repeat the things
I shouldn't hear

So don't come near me
or put out your hand
because I'll pick you
if I can
pickyou
pickyou
if I can

I want to be Free
Can't You Understand

Grace Nichols

This reminds me of a parrot that bit me.

Badgers

Badgers come creeping from dark under ground,
Badgers scratch hard with a bristly sound,
Badgers go nosing around.

Badgers have whiskers and black and white faces,
Badger cubs scramble and scrap and run races,
Badgers like overgrown places.

Badgers don't jump when a vixen screams,
Badgers drink quietly from moonshiny streams,
Badgers dig holes in our dreams.

Badgers are working while you and I sleep,
Pushing their tunnels down twisting and steep,
Badgers have secrets to keep.

Richard Edwards

At the Bottom of the Garden

No, it isn't an old football
grown all shrunken and prickly
because it was left out so long
at the bottom of the garden.

It's only Hedgehog
who, when she thinks I'm not looking,
unballs herself to move…
Like bristling black lightning.

Grace Nichols

Squirrel

With a rocketing rip
Squirrel will zip
Up a tree-bole
As if down a hole.

He jars to a stop
With tingling ears.
He has two gears:
Freeze and top.

Then up again, plucky
As a jockey
Galloping a Race–
–Horse
Into space.

Ted Hughes

Giraffes

Giraffes
   I like them.
   Ask me why.
        Because they hold their heads up high.
        Because their necks stretch to the sky.
        Because they're quiet calm and shy.
        Because they run so fast they fly.
        Because their eyes are velvet brown.
        Because their coats are spotted tan.
        Because they eat the tops of trees.
        Because their legs have knobbly knees.
        Because
        Because. That's why
I like giraffes.

Mary Ann Hoberman

   I love giraffes too!

The Panther

The panther is like a leopard,
Except it hasn't been peppered.
Should you behold a panther crouch,
Prepare to say Ouch.
Better yet, if called by a panther,
Don't anther.

Ogden Nash

This always makes me laugh.

The Year

January started it
February frosted it
March blew it
April showered it
May sprung it
June gave it roses
July took it on holiday
August heat waved it
September grew it fruit salad
October put its coat on
November fogged it
December waved it goodbye.

Julie Holder

I like the way each month is described.

Recipe for Spring

Some sunny, warm days,
a soft-bustling breeze.

Scatterings of swallows
and greening of trees.

White, puffy clouds
in a bluebell sky.

Rain sprinkling freshness.
A splash in my eye!

Ducklings and daisies
and buzzing of bees.

Blustery beaches
and freshly-made cheese.

Off to the park,
to run, slide, and swing.

It's the best of all seasons,
welcome back, Spring!

Joan Poulson

This poem makes me feel warm inside, so does spring.

Fireworks

Fire sticks shoot through billowing black,
Ice-creamy sparkles tumble and crack,
Red carnations whistle and spin,
Everyone cheers as fireworks begin.
Wood piled high is eaten by flame.
On top Guy Fawkes get roasted again,
Rockets return, blackened to ash,
Kaleidoscope colours collide and clash,
Somewhere a screech, and somewhere a crash.

Steve Turner

> I feel like I am watching a real fireworks show.

Autumn Is …

A shadow tall
A splash of gold
A day cut short
One playground, cold.

A conker race
A crunch of feet,
A lazy wasp
One fireside treat.

A tree left bare
A classroom BRIGHT
A flower folding
One morning, white.

A sinking sun
A painted world,
A robin's song
One hedgehog, curled.

A silver mist
A cobweb's crown
A picture postcard
Golden brown.

Andrew Collett

Winter

Whirling snow and whistling wind
Icy patterns on window panes
Numb fingers and freezing toes
Trees stripped bare
Earth bone-hard
Roaring fires and long, dark nights.

John Foster

This reminds me how cold
and bleak winter is.

December Leaves

The fallen leaves are cornflakes
That fill the lawn's wide dish,
And night and noon
The wind's a spoon
That stirs them with a swish.

The sky's a silver sifter
A-sifting white and slow,
That gently shakes
On crisp brown flakes
The sugar known as snow.

Kaye Starbird

The Greedy Monster

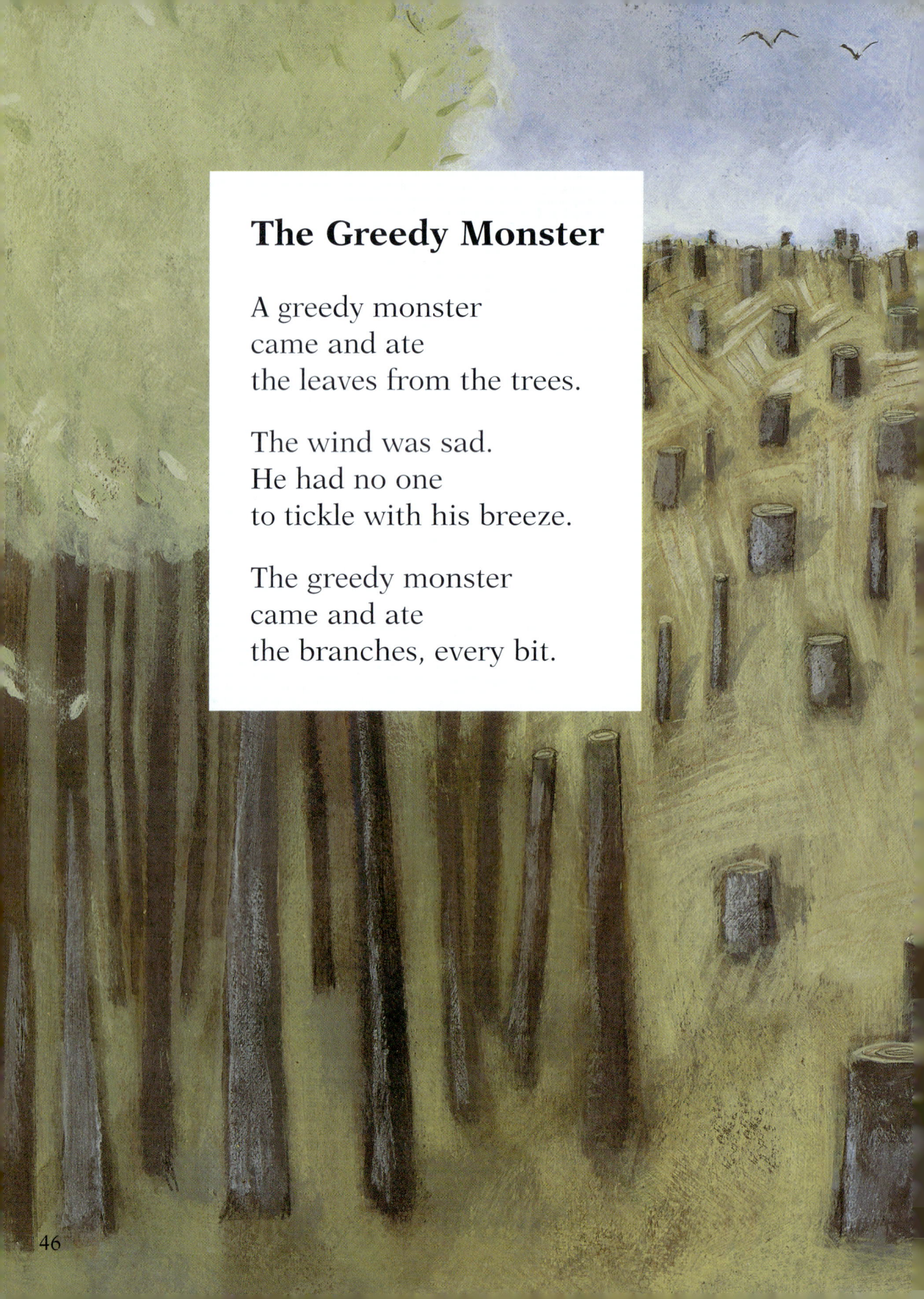

A greedy monster
came and ate
the leaves from the trees.

The wind was sad.
He had no one
to tickle with his breeze.

The greedy monster
came and ate
the branches, every bit.

The birds flew sulky
in the sky;
they had nowhere to sit.

The monster
ate the forest,
trunks and roots, in a day.

Now houses stand
where the forest stood,
and the birds have gone away.

Irene Rawnsley

This poem makes me cross because I feel very strongly about destroying the countryside.

Dreamer

I dreamt I was an ocean
and no one polluted me.

I dreamt I was a whale
and no hunters chased after me.

I dreamt I was the air
and nothing blackened me.

I dreamt I was a stream
and nobody poisoned me.

I dreamt I was an elephant
and nobody stole my ivory.

I dreamt I was a rain forest
and no one cut down my trees.

I dreamt I painted a smile
on the face of the Earth
for all to see.

Brian Moses

This makes me think how important it is to care for the environment.

A Letter to the Alphabet

Dear Alphabet,
        I'd like to say, thanks, for the words you give away. From Aardvarks to Zebras, from millions to noughts your twenty six letters calculate thoughts. I can read what is written, I can write what I say, I can picture with words in every way.

This is thin

This is fat

this is bumpy bumpy bumpy bumpy bumpyy bumpyy bumpyy bumpyy bumpyy bummmpyy

This is flat

THIS IS HAPPY

This is sad

This is good

This is bad

this is writing on a wall

and this is the alphabet
ABCDEFGHIJKLM
NOPQRSTUVWXYZ

that says it all.

Julie Holder

Rhythm Machine

Soft and Strumming —

LOUD and Strumming —

Listen to that NEAT refrain!

Add a TRUMPET

And a DRUM kit —

Why not change the BEAT again?

UP THE VOLUME

Eardrum priser,

INSTANT POP GROUP synthesIZER!

Trevor Harvey

Guess Who Haiku (Creatures)

Neck which stretches high,
Patchwork skin in brown and gold,
A strange sight running.

Arachnid by name,
Enemy to careless flies,
Known to persevere.

Small furry mammal,
Long, radar ears, twitching nose,
Often called Peter.

Uninvited guests,
Small, scurrying night raiders,
Addicted to cheese.

Daphne Kitching

Riddle Me Hot, Riddle Me Cold

My first is in fish, but not in bone.
My second in iron, but not in stone.
My third in crown and also in throne.
My fourth once in twice,
But twice in returned.
Touch me, get burned!

My first is in wish, but not in bone.
My second is in rock, but not in stone.
My third once in twice,
But twice in tease.
Touch me and freeze!

John Foster

I enjoy puzzling out riddles.

The Land of the Bumbley Boo

In the Land of the Bumbley Boo
The people are red, white and blue,
They never blow noses,
Or even wear closes,
What a sensible thing to do!

In the Land of the Bumbley Boo
You can buy lemon pie at the Zoo;
They give away Foxes
In little Pink Boxes
And Bottles of Dandylion Stew.

In the Land of the Bumbley Boo
You never see a Gnu,
But thousands of cats
Wearing trousers and hats
Made of Pumpkins and Pelican Glue!

Chorus

Oh, the Bumbley Boo! The Bumbley Boo!
That's the place for me and you!
So hurry! Let's run!
The train leaves at one!
For the Land of the Bumbley Boo!
The wonderful Bumbley Boo-Boo-Boo!
The Wonderful Bumbley BOO!!!

Spike Milligan

Tongue Twisters

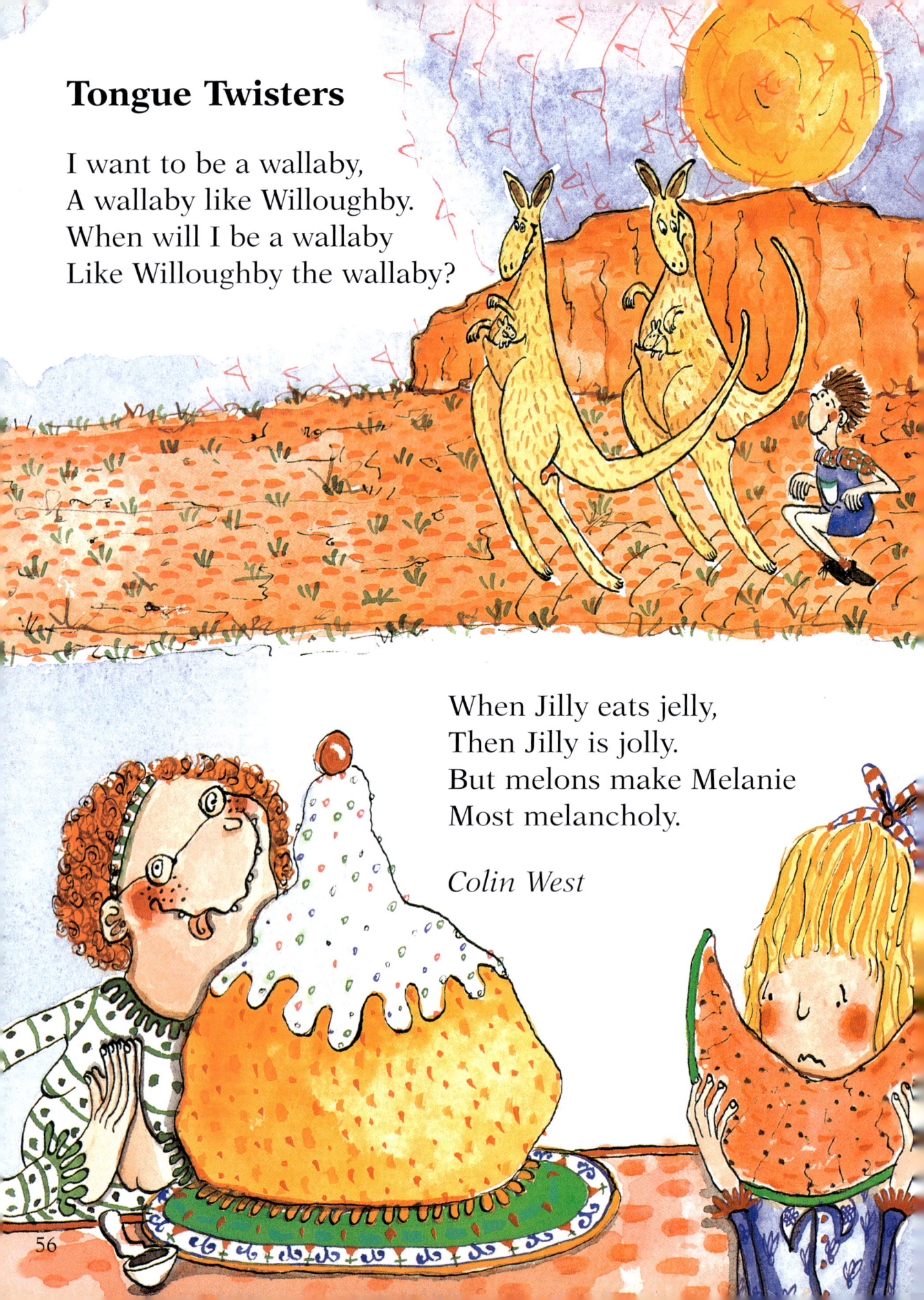

I want to be a wallaby,
A wallaby like Willoughby.
When will I be a wallaby
Like Willoughby the wallaby?

When Jilly eats jelly,
Then Jilly is jolly.
But melons make Melanie
Most melancholy.

Colin West

Shaun Short's Short Shorts

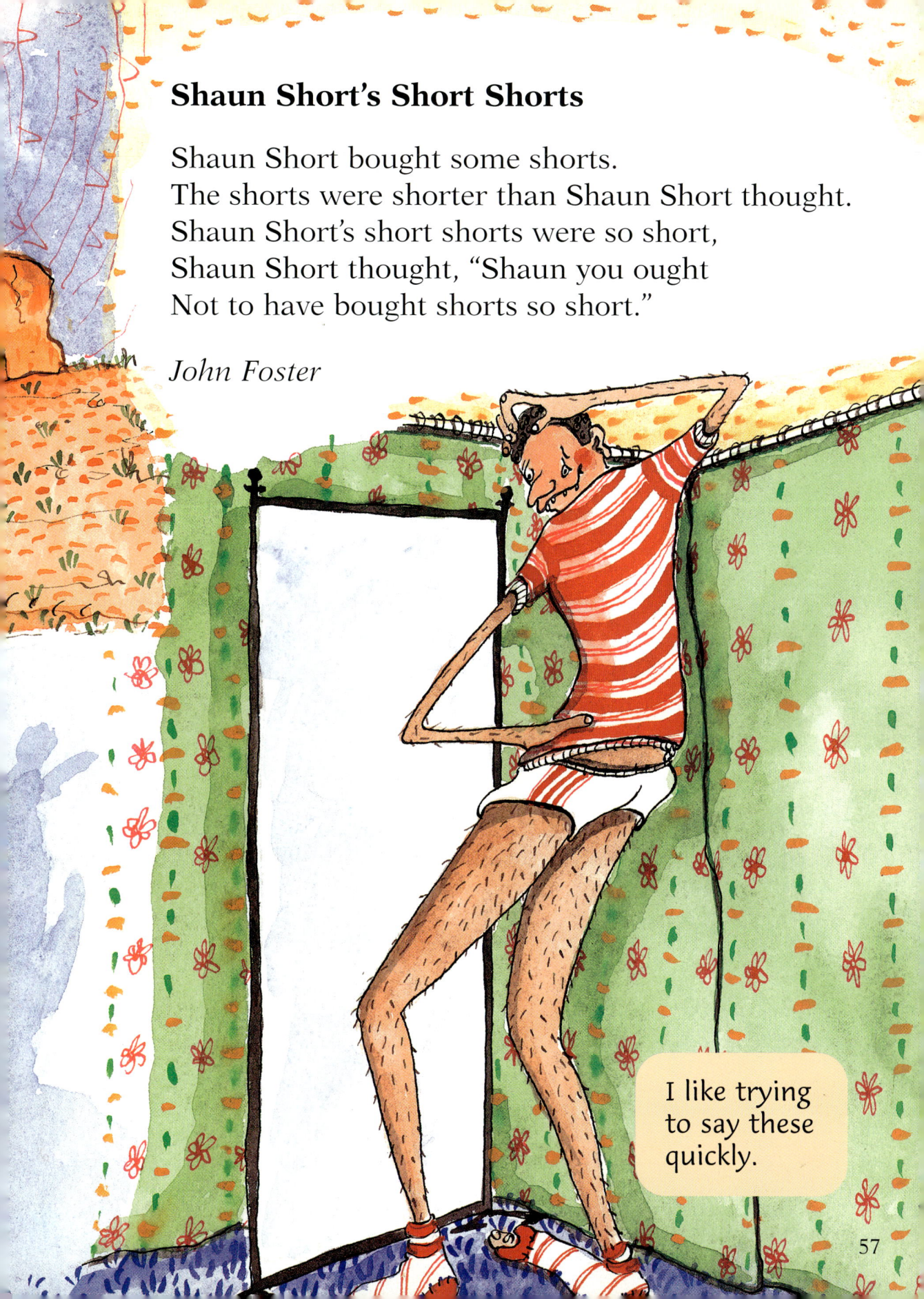

Shaun Short bought some shorts.
The shorts were shorter than Shaun Short thought.
Shaun Short's short shorts were so short,
Shaun Short thought, "Shaun you ought
Not to have bought shorts so short."

John Foster

I like trying to say these quickly.

A Famous Painter

A famous painter
Met his death
Because he couldn't
Draw his breath.

Anon

There was an Old Man of Blackheath

There was an old man of Blackheath,
Who sat on his set of false teeth,
   Said he, with a start,
     "Oh, Lord, bless my heart!
I've bitten myself underneath!"

Anon

Little Miss Fidget

She fiddled with the stereo,
The washer and the phone.
Anything with dials on
Was in her fiddle zone.
But now her hands are bandaged up,
She's resting for a while.
She did not read the sign that said:
"Don't touch the croc-o-dial."

Bill Condon

I love funny poems like these.

Some Favourite Words

Mugwump, chubby, dunk and whoa,
Swizzle, doom and snoop,
Flummox, lilt and afterglow,
Gruff, bamboozle, whoop
And nincompoop.

Wallow, jungle, lumber, sigh,
Ooze and zodiac,
Innuendo, lullaby,
Ramp and mope and quack
And paddywhack.

Moony, undone, lush and bole,
Inkling, tusk, guffaw,
Waspish, croon and cubbyhole,
Fern, fawn, dumbledore
And many more…

Richard Edwards

Index of First Lines

A custard coloured	12
A famous painter	58
A greedy monster	46
A shadow tall	43
A white face	6
An aeroplane climbs	11
As big as a ball	10
As I was coming to school, Sir	22
Badgers come creeping from dark under ground	36
Butterflies	8
Crash and clang!	16
Dear Alphabet	50
Eatable ear-rings	12
Fire sticks shoot through billowing black	42
Flip flop	28
Giraffes	38
Granny Granny	24
I asked the little boy who cannot see	14
I can get through the doorway without any key	9
I dreamt I was an ocean	48
I like to stay up	26
I love the	18
I must go down to the seas again	29
I want to be a wallaby	56
I'm a parrot	34

In the Land of the Bumbley Boo	54
January started it	40
Mugwump, chubby, dunk, and whoa	60
My first is in fish, but not in bone	53
Neck which stretches high	52
No, it isn't an old football	37
On a breezy day	9
pink is a marshmallow whisper	15
Saris hang on the washing line	13
Shaun Short bought some shorts	57
She fiddled with the stereo	59
Slowly, silently, now the moon	5
Small reed fringed pools	12
Soft and humming	51
Some sunny, warm days	41
The alleyway is crooked	20
The fallen leaves are cornflakes	45
The panther is like a leopard	39
There was an old man of Blackheath	58
When Jilly eats jelly	56
When the rain first started it was just a shower	30
Whirling snow and whistling wind	44
Who has seen the wind?	8
With a rocketing rip	37

Acknowledgements

The editor and publisher are grateful for permission to include the following poems:

Allan Ahlberg: 'As I was Coming to School' from *Please Mrs Butler*, (Kestrel, 1983), © Allan Ahlberg 1983, reprinted by permission of Penguin Books Ltd; **Ann Bonner:** 'The Moon' first published in *My First Has Gone Bonkers* editedby Brian Moses (Blackie, 1993), reprinted by permission of the author; **Debjani Chatterjee:** 'My Sari' first published in *Read Me: A Poem A Day* for the National Year of Reading edited by Gaby Morgan, (Macmillan Children's Books, 1998), reprinted by permission of the author; **Andrew Collett:** 'Autumn is…', © Andrew Collett 2000, first published in this collection by permission of the author; **John Cotton:** 'Definitions', © John Cotton 2000, first published in this collection by permission of the author; **Iain Crichton-Smith:** 'On a Breezy Day', © Iain Crichton-Smith 2000, first published in this collection by permission of Donalda G Smith; **Walter de la Mare:** 'Silver' from *The Complete Poems of Walter de la Mare* (UK 1979, USA1970), reprinted by permission of The Literary Trustees of Walter de la Mare and the Society of Authors as their representative; **Gina Douthwaite:** 'Ambitious Aeroplane' from *Picture a Poem* (Hutchinson, 1994), © Gina Douthwaite 1994, reprinted by permission of the author; **Richard Edwards:** 'Badgers', from *The Word Party* (Puffin); 'The Alleyway', from *Leopards on Mars* (Viking); 'Some Favourite Words', from *Whispers From a Wardrobe* (Lutterworth),all reprinted by permission of the author; **Eleanor Farjeon:** 'J is for Jazzman' from *Silver Sand and Snow* (Michael Joseph), reprinted by permission of David Higham Associates Ltd; **John Foster:** 'Winter', © John Foster 1995, first published in *Standing on the Sidelines* (OUP); 'Shaun Short's Short Shorts', © John Foster 1997, first published in *Tongue Twisters and Tonsil Twizzlers* edited by Paul Cookson (Macmillan); 'Riddle Me Hot, Riddle Me Cold', © John Foster 2000, first published in this collection, all reprinted by permission of the author; **Trevor Harvey:** 'Rhythm Machine', © Trevor Harvey 1994, first published in *Techno Talk* (Bodley Head, 1994), reprinted by permission of the author; **Mary Ann Hoberman:** 'Giraffes' from *The Llama Who Had No Pajama* by Mary Ann Hoberman (Browndeer Press/Harcourt Brace, 1973, 1998), © Mary Ann Hoberman 1973, 1998, reprinted by permission of Gina Maccoby Literary Agency; **Julie Holder:** 'The Year' and 'A Letter to the Alphabet', both © Julie Holder 2000, first published in this collection by permission of the author; **Ted Hughes:** 'Squirrel' from *The Cat and The Cuckoo* (Sunstone Press, 1987), reprinted by permission of Faber & Faber Ltd; **Daphne Kitching:** 'Guess Who Haiku', © Daphne Kitching 2000, first publishedin this collection by permission of the author; **John Masefield:** 'Sea Fever', reprinted by permission of The Society of Authors as the Literary Representatives of the Estate of John Masefield; **Spike Milligan:** 'The Land of the Bumbley Boo', © Spike Milligan, from *Silly Verse for Kids* (Puffin), reprinted by permission of Spike Milligan Productions; **Brian Moses:** 'Dreamer' first published in *Hippopotamus Dancing and Other Poems* (CUP, 1994), reprinted by permission of the author; **Ogden Nash:** 'The Panther', © 1940 Ogden Nash, from *Verses from 1929 On* (Little Brown and Co, 1942), also from *Candy is Dandy: The Best of Ogden Nash* (Andre Deutsch) reprinted by permission of Curtis Brown Ltd, New York, and Andre Deutsch; **Grace Nichols:** 'I'm a Parrot', 'I'd Like to Stay Up' and 'Granny Granny Please Comb My Hair' from *Come On Into My Tropical Garden* (Black Publishers), © Grace Nichols 1988; 'At the Bottom of the Garden', from *Asana and the Animals* (Walker Books), © Grace Nichols 1997, all reprinted by permission of Curtis Brown Ltd, London, on behalf of Grace Nichols; **Jack Ousbey:** 'The Mighty Ark', © Jack Ousbey 2000, first published in this collection by permission of the author; **Joan Poulson:** 'Recipe for Spring', © Joan Poulson 2000, first published in this collection by permission of the author; **Irene Rawnsley:** 'The Greedy Monster', © Irene Rawnsley 1991, first published in *The Green Umbrella* (A C Black, 1991), reprinted by permission of the author; **James Reeves:** 'The Wind' from *Complete Poems for Children* (Heinemann), © James Reeves, reprinted by permission of Laura Cecil Literary Agency on behalf of the James Reeves Estate; **Steve Turner:** 'Fireworks' from *The Day I Fell Down the Toilet and Other Poems* (Lion Publishing), reprinted by permission of the publisher; **Celia Warren:** 'Pink is a Marshmallow Whisper', © Celia Warren 2000, first published in this collection by permission of the author; **Colin West:** 'I Want to be a Wallaby' and 'When Jilly Eats Jelly', both © Colin West 1982, from *Not to be Taken Seriously* (Hutchinson, 1982), reprinted by permission of the author

Although we have tried to trace and contact holders before publication, in some cases this has not been possible. If contacted we will be pleased to rectify any errors or omissions at the earliest opportunity.

The Artists

Peter Bailey pp 50–51;
Debbie Boon pp 24–25, 34–35, 40–41;
Matthew Buckingham pp 42–43;
Charlotte Combe pp 30–33;
Abigail Conway pp 46–47;
Graham Cox pp 22–23;
Emma Garner pp 6–7;
Charlotte Hard pp 16–17;
Sue Heap pp 26–27;
Anna Hopkins pp 36–37, 60–61;

Neal Layton pp 10–11, 38–39;
Alan Marks pp 28–29;
Jill Newton pp 14–15;
Joanne Partis pp 12–13;
Liz Pichon pp 18–19, 42–43;
Nick Schon pp 58–59;
Linda Schwab pp 8–9, 44–45;
Lisa Smith pp 52–53;
Gary Taylor pp 5, 48–49;
Doffy Weir pp 20–21, 54–55;